John Henry's
Partner Speaks

John Henry's Partner Speaks

Poems by David Salner

WordTech Editions

Published by WordTech Editions
P.O. Box 541106
Cincinnati, OH 45254-1106

ISBN: 9781934999110
LCCN: 2008927896

Poetry Editor: Kevin Walzer
Business Editor: Lori Jareo

Visit us on the web at www.wordtechweb.com

COVER PHOTO: "John and Phil" by David Salner
from the wood carvings by Charlie Permelia, courtesy
Dwarfus Permelia, Lester, WV

Acknowledgments

I would like to thank the Puffin Foundation, Ltd., for a grant that helped make it possible for me to write the last section of this book, *John Henry's Partner Speaks*, which first appeared as a chapbook of the same name from Pudding House. I would also like to thank the Summers County Library in Hinton, WV, for the use of their valuable files on John Henry, as well as Professor Jack C. Wills for his help.

(Just to forestall a question I'm frequently asked: the Phil Henderson tapes do not exist; Phil is my invention.)

Some of these poems appeared in the chapbooks *The Chosen* (Pudding House) and *Mug Shots* (March Street Press). In addition to these presses, I would like to credit the following journals for first publishing poems in this book:

5 AM: "At Hawks Nest, WV"
Appalachian Journal: "Dr. Raines" and "The Whip" (appearing
    here as "In Dade Coal Mine")
Baltimore Review: "The Machinist and the Cell Phone" (also in *To Be This Man*, Swan Scythe Press)
Borderlands: "Creation" and "Firpo"
Cimarron Review: "Lou Gehrig at the MDA Clinic in Morgantown, WV"
Elixir: "Melville, Dreaming," "Rain on Plastic," "On a Bench at
    the Cortlandt Street Pier," and "Monongah, WV" (also in
    Coal: a Poetry Anthology, Blair Mountain Press)
ForPoetry.com: "The New World"
Green Mountains Review: "On a Triumph 650"
Hurricane Review: "The Legacy"
Illuminations: "Reality Childhood"
International Poetry Review: "August 6, 1945"
Margie/The American Journal of Poetry: "A Short Poem on the Shooting by
    Police of Charquisa Johnson in Washington, DC"
Minnesota Review: "Furnace Tenders at Dawn" and "Summer
    Words"
Natural Bridge: "Spinless"
North American Review: "Guadalupe, AZ."
North Dakota Quarterly: "False Identities"
Parting Gifts: "Tennis Ball Strikes," "A Father's Lesson," and "An

Unfinished Poem for Lou Gehrig."
Poet Lore: "Opening Day"
Poetry Depth Quarterly: "Two Girls, Fishing"
Potomac Review: "The Seventy-ninth Miner"
Prairie Schooner: "Blue Grass Poem" and "American Poem"
South Carolina Review: "A Letter from the U.P. Line"
South Dakota Review: "Wyoming" and "Never Leaving Duluth"
Southern Humanities Review: "Beyond Gypsy"
Southern Poetry Review: for Every Cab Driver Has a Story
Spillway: "Magnesium" and "Coming Home from Hoot-Owl
    Shift"
Texas Review: "When I Was a Thing"
The Literary Review: "Furnace"
Threepenny Review: "In Another Mug Shot" (also in *Poetry Daily*)
Washington Square: "The Reader Is a Clerk from Salvador"
Witness: "My Father Catches Me Off-Guard"

I would like to single out my wife, Barbara, and daughter, Lily, for their support and encouragement.

This book is dedicated to the working people of West Virginia, who are heirs to a proud history. I am honored to have spent many years working in their midst.

Contents

Part I. *When I Was a Thing*

In Another Mug Shot

The camera picked up
the light on the plastic
of my fake leather jacket.
Also, my hair was too long
and my mustache
gave me the shifty look
often found in mug shots.
In fact, it was a mug shot
taken in the basement
of the Hall of Justice
in 1968—or Injustice
as we called it. Now,
it's almost December
2002, and I'm getting ready
to welcome my daughter
home from college. My hair
is shorter and my beard
neatly clipped, but the
mug shot would come out
with the same shifty look.
The change is in something else—
not in the way I look or
the suit jacket I'm wearing
instead of fake leather—
but in the background
of the mug shot. Can you
see it—the war taking shape?
It shines like a new war,
like only a new war can.

Beyond Gypsy

They invented the guitar—
which is simply an instrument
that can only be played at night—and songs
with words that make Arabian horses
cry in their stables. Some people
considered the *Gypsies* outcasts
but in fact they're the mortar
holding humanity together—lifting
a punch line from one province
and grafting it to a joke
from a far off town, or sprinkling
a spice for pork—in one clan's recipe—
on the lamb of a distant tribe,
or vice versa. Like birds, they weave
pieces of colored ribbon through a nest of twigs and put
a *Gypsy* twist on everything.

Some of their best work is accomplished
through casting a *Gypsy* spell. This is what
I had in mind when I asked a friend
if a certain public figure
could be bewitched into telling the truth. "It's
been tried before," he said—
"and just won't work—like putting Paprika
on ice cream or sherbet—
some things are beyond *Gyspy*."

The New World

I have been imagining how my grandmother
would have left Hungary, with only a sweater
to cover her bones, squinting at the sun
in the haze of the ocean, as her new husband
plays something like a guitar, but smaller.

She joins him in a chorus about a horse
who responds to the touch of a Gypsy trainer
but not the whip of the Hungarian master.
These newlyweds left in a hurry, carrying only
the little guitar and the old gray sweater.

The wind whips over the great steel decks
as she tells a joke about the subtle difference
between luck and fortune. They squint at a spot
suspended over the ocean. Even I see it—
that opal haze, brilliant with vagueness.

Opening Day

I helped the sexton's son, Russell,
bury old Ginny Mummert one day in mid-April.
I remember the softness of the spring air and the hint
of manure from somebody spreading maybe a mile off.
It was opening day, and the Orioles were on the air.
We put the portable radio by the water jug
and draped the antenna over somebody's stone,
but we couldn't hear much except static
and the sound of dirt on the casket.

We were almost done with Ginny
when the Orioles got runners on base
in the eighth inning—so we stopped our work
and hovered over the radio, listening hard
for each crackling word. And if you didn't know
we were pulling for Gus Triandos to hit the long ball,
you might have thought it was our gentle send-off
for Ginny. Godspeed. But the Birds never scored.

Spinless

As a kid I played softball for the church team.
We weren't Lutheran, but I could hit line drives
and there was a shortage of men under forty.
So they batted me fifth and tried to convert me
between innings. When they stopped talking about

life after death, our record improved.
We had that chatter and team chemistry
which is the greater good in softball, church or not.
Opposing batters couldn't touch our pitcher,
old Carroll Lenhardt, head of the school board.

He often complained of arthritis, but he was a different man
in a ball game, pitching all day in his bibs
as easy as some people sleep in their skin.
He would chew the same cigar for a whole game
while grinning down bad boys from the other team.

Then one day in July, I surprised myself
more than anyone else, by quitting the team.
No hard feelings, I attended the last game
to root for the church. Carroll, the same cigar
in his teeth, tossed unhittable floaters

that hung there, spinless, in the evening air.

Tennis-Ball Strikes

I had the fast ball and the curve
to become a good pitcher, but lacked control.
So I chalked a strike zone on the wall of the church
and practiced throwing tennis-ball strikes
to Mickey Mantle and other great hitters.

I was deep in the count, when I noticed
my dog trying to play with the sexton's hen.
A cloud of brown feathers went up,
and the dog looked guilty
before the hen hit the ground.

I knew what had to be done
when your dog killed chickens. It was
every farm boy's nightmare—and a test
that you're fit for this hard life. I thought
of the tales on the churchyard stones:

of war, hard childbirth, and deadly flu.
In a cold world, I armed myself
for a cold deed. Then my Dad found out
he was being fired from his job
and we moved to the city.

A Father's Lesson

A skinny man, he looks ferocious
dancing over the grease marks in our garage
holding his fists like rocks in front of his face.
"Keep your head down," my father says,
as he scuffles and strikes at the air
with sudden vengeance. "Keep away from him
until you see his nose, then sock him
hard—never pull your punches."

The next day, I use his advice on Harold,
the school-yard bully, who screamed
running away from PS 87.

When my father was fifteen, he got a factory job
in one of those tough Hungarian towns
near Pittsburgh. A big guy pushed him down
and rubbed his face on the floor. My father
waited until the big guy lowered his head
to the drinking fountain, then he picked up a shovel
and bashed him with everything he had
in that skinny body, driving the nose
into the steel fountain so that blood and water
splashed over the wall. "Don't fight fair,"
my father tells me. "If someone wants to fight fair
you won't have to fight him."

I think back to the bullies in offices
who baited my father, witch-hunted him, drove him
out of his job to a nervous breakdown.
They never came out in the open—and my father,
looking half-punch-drunk from wine and gin,
never knew what hit him.

"The nose has so many nerve-endings,"
my father tells me. "Even a brave man will cry
when he's hit there, and bullies aren't brave."
Years later, I have a clear shot

at Harold's nose and drive my fist
even harder now. That's for my father.

Reality Childhood

Baltimore MD.

1.

"Hey, Mister!" my friends and I yelled
as he stomped down Chelsea Terrace,
"You just have one leg!" We ran after him
not knowing enough to be amazed
that he could keep up with a garbage truck
or that he had to. We were five-years old,
astounded at his peg-leg as he hurried
down Chelsea Terrace, hoisting cans,
ragging sweat from his eyes. "Hey Mister!"
we yelled, as the truck pulled away, and he
broke into a wondrous staccato run.

2.

The loudest noise I ever heard
was the air-raid siren on PS 87.
When I first learned about the bomb,
I asked my parents
if Japanese children
had such a siren
and if it worked as well.

3.

The Ambassador,
on Liberty Heights in Baltimore,
was my first movie theater.

Cartoons began at noon
before the Saturday double-feature,

which always included a movie
starring either John Wayne, Tyrone Power,
or Maureen O'Hara—if not all three—
in brilliant color. My new reality
was the green of O'Hara's dress and eyes
against her chestnut hair. It wasn't
loveliness or sex I thought of
back then, but the wonder of color.

We emerged from the Ambassador
into the unreal sound of traffic, the uncinematic
grinding and hissing. Blinded by the afternoon sun,
we felt our giddy way home.

But what was the other reality—
the one across town
in the colored movie theater?

The Legacy

I'm still finding the tools you left me:
a wooden level with a yellow eye,
to see if I'm half a bubble off; a set
of ignition wrenches, bird-sized,
to go with the bird-sized arms that run
in the Salner family; a collop of lead,
cold and gray, to steady a hammer blow;
a drill with a knob you lean your gut into
while you turn the crank-handle; wood chisels,
plumb-bobs, a can of carpenter's pencils.
When I use them, I hear your parched voice
over my shoulder—and your judgment,
which I can't escape: "Measure twice, cut once."

My Father Catches Me Off-Guard

He waits for me like a child on our front steps,
a little afraid but proud when I tousle his hair.
"What are you doing here, Dad?" I ask. His eyes
widen with awe, and I realize he has finally
accepted me. Accept? He worships me.

I put my briefcase in the hall. How he sniffs
at the leather! How his eyes grow large
as they feast on the papers inside! His stubby fingers
stroke my overcoat as I try to take it off.
Hair tonic, smoke, and the brusque scent

of shoe polish—he loves the smells I bring home
from a day at the office. Gone is the way
he looked down his nose at my unlettered friends,
my shabby clothes, or the jobs doing manual trades.
He no longer corrects my failure to use the subjunctive,

as if grammar *was* the most important thing in his life.
In fact, I have no idea what's important to him.
Perhaps I should take him outside, in the summer breeze
that stirs wistfully around our old house,
and teach him to ride a bike or throw a football.

Just when I feel I can loosen my tie and have a cocktail,
my father, this vulnerable child, walks toward me,
uncertainty lighting his eyes, two futures in every step.

Choice

It's a wonderful thing to have a mother
you didn't come from. I can remember—
when I was four—the heavy varnish on the floor
I was playing on in one of those apartments
built all over Baltimore
after the war. My mother
holds me in the glitter of her black eyes
expressing humor easily, strength and care, and love
with difficulty. She has my father there
for back-up. It's a conversation
filled with produce words—"We picked you out,"
as if I were an avocado and they were squeezing
my chubby knees—or a cantaloupe.
My mother sniffs my bellybutton
while the world looks on. "We'll take this one,"
she announces, "because he's ripe."
Both of them are smoking, and the words
parade in the smoke, dance in the air
high overhead, meaningless as motes
                                    —for I had already
adopted my mother, when she was a girl
about my age, playing on the marble steps
in a neighborhood where poor Jews lived
in row houses. My orthodox grandmother had a painting
of a handsome man, her husband, who disappeared
when his bank failed. They never saw him again.
As I stared at the painting, I understood
my father would disappear, also,
in a way my mother never would. The words
meant nothing to me, for my mother's eyes
had already told me what I had to know.
I was not the fruit of her body but of something
more important—her choice.
I was the fruit of a woman's choice.

August 6, 1945

A year and a day after I was born
President Truman was hit by the bomb
meant for Hiroshima.

All across the island
people came out of their shelters. They were all there—
the all-night partiers and the night-shift workers,
every *indispensable* one of them. Even the teen-agers
were there (although their only special gift
was sleeping in and being themselves
in Hiroshima, as in other cities).

There would be no need to float candles
into the rivers each August—
for the babies of Hiroshima were there,
laughing beside us
about false-alarms and rescues.

A year and a day after I was born,
Hiroshima still stood
among the islands of Japan.
President Truman had taken the bomb.

False Identities

Many bought documents underground
only to find that the papers were real
and therefore wouldn't work. Only one
crossed the border in a mask
of Victor Mature. The guards checked their records
and waved him in. A hay wagon hid one
as the border guards probed with their bayonets
in the loose hay. Did he avoid the rummaging blades?
The wagon went on, so we'll never know.
The untouchables tried to disguise themselves
as the unfeeling, but they were betrayed
by their emotions, when they saw someone suffering.
Some disguised themselves as saints.
The guards let them pass for it was a ruse.
But when a man without sin approached,
the guards locked him up, for he was
what he was—and that was a crime
in this borderland world. Some people
thought those were most daring who stole
pieces of false identity and bluffed their way
across the border and into a new life.
But in fact, the most daring were those
who told the truth about the border:
how it forced them to hide what is best
in themselves, behind false papers;
to live without the pleasure
of being discovered for who they are;
to die without love and a kiss—
though they might be only yards away
just behind a wall or across a river,
in a part of themselves they might never find.

A Short Poem on the Shooting By Police Of Charquisa Johnson, April 27, 2003, in Washington, DC

The police said she held a gun in the air
and refused to drop it. Her friend
said her hands were empty
except for the kiss she was blowing
her two children. They blew her lights out
but missed what was dangerous to them—
there it is, still blowing—
Charquisa's kiss.

Melville, Dreaming

If I eat papaya and bittersweet chocolate
within an hour of bedtime, I'll dream
of sailing a catamaran beyond the reef
and into a sea too wide for my own good.
It's gentle, which can be deceiving.

If I sip on cocoa and eat apple crisp
I'll dream of an old-fashioned kitchen
and an attractive woman with a streak of
white hair. Cruella DeVille?
We'll have sex unless someone wakes me.

A shot of gin and I'll dream of a pub
in London, circa 1835. Another shot
and I'll feel guilty, but—hell!
I'm a weaver in the mills, carrying the empire
all these years. I'll have another shot.

But when sheets of icy rain
fall on the city and the water courses, tea-brown,
down gutters and into sewers—
I realize that I'm susceptible
to a recurring dream in which a well-dressed chap

stares at me and pronounces the words,
"Ah, Bartleby! Ah, Humanity!"

Rain on Plastic

I look up at the blue tarpaulin
and hear the rain on plastic. I can't
remember how often I've camped out
in the rain—it's one of those things
you don't keep a record of—but this time
Herman Melville, the customs clerk,
sits in the chair beside me. He tells me
about his one success, *Typee,* a memoir
of deserting a whaler and finding safety
among cannibals. "And then the critics
did me in," Melville says. And I: "Of course—
you said cannibals were better than Christians!"

Melville laughs as if he hadn't thought of this,
and we sit there—two clerks, listening
to rain on plastic all day long.

On a Bench at the Cortlandt Street Pier

". . . those delightful days, before my father became a bankrupt . . ."
—Herman Melville, *Redburn*

We can hear the creaking of the boats
moored in the darkness. Father and son
are waiting to leave this almost-island
for someplace where the father will lose
more money than he lost before. The little boy
moans with cold and tries to dream
of an island whose name he can't pronounce,
but which we know, today, as Nuka Hiva.
There he will become a captive of the very
adventure he is weaving. Then he will join
a mutiny and escape, with difficulty,
from a prison without bars. His last dream—
of becoming a beachcomber—breaks
upon the wind-blade of the sun. Waking up,
he can feel his father fussing beside him,
trying to keep the little boy warm.
The wind kicks spray, blows trash,
and flaps the sign, hanging above them:
DEPARTURES FOR ALBANY
—TICKET HOLDERS ONLY

Creation and Firpo

After a painting by George Bellows

According to the Big Bang theory
the universe was born with a sound
that you can hear to this day
if you try not to listen for it.

I heard it in a bar in Trenton
as I stared at a painting of the giant Firpo
knocking Dempsey from the ring
into my lap like a stunned bird.

The moment was full of exploding stars.

The Reader Is a Clerk from Salvador, Poet a Sightless Man

I've been entering and leaving like this
rehearsing a few words of Spanish, hoping
you'll guide me from the milk to the counter
and that you'll answer back
with words that I can hold like pegs
driven into the sheer face of the silence.

I enter the store and climb into the story
of how you were chased through another market
with your brother, who is really pudgy—
I can tell from the way that your voice
caresses the silence when you say *Gordito*
at the same time your hands must be rubbing

the great belly of the air. Anyway, *Gordito*
comes whirling around a huge vat of peppers
and falls into the lap of someone important.
—And then you stop and look at your
dumb, gesturing hands because I can't
see them. And in this moment when disbelief

breaks, I stumble against the deli case,
which contains cheese and sausage and maybe
something like a goat-head with an eye
staring lightlessly back at mine—and you
hug me away from the danger
laughing and scolding in Spanish as if we were

brothers in another market, ten-thousand miles away.
I thank you for the milk
and enter the sidewalk, which is like
entering a river with other boats.

An Unfinished Poem for Lou Gehrig

Nothing could be more difficult
than to write a poem about you.
Let me begin with the shoes you couldn't tie . . .

A Letter from the U.P. Line

(from a passenger, shortly after its completion)

Dear Martha,
        As we pulled into Omaha—
such smoke and such confusion!

The conductor warned us, in his deepest bass—
a band of hostile Indians were on the tracks.
(He got it from General Sheridan himself.)
I thought of you and Todd and little Russell,
back in Harrisburg, with only $100—
and a side of beef. "Fortunately, I double
as an agent for THE GREAT OCCIDENTAL
INSURANCE AND UNDERWRITING CO.,"
the conductor boomed. "For just $7.00—
and $2 telegraphing fee—I can write a policy
that pays $500. Indian attacks are covered—
just 50 cents more." More dust.
The train topped out at 20 mph and everything—
stream beds, rocks, and trees—was full of dust,
and dust was all I saw for many miles. I saw
some Indians go limping
from a burnt-out camp—
two young ones and a squaw, who pulled
their household on a wheel-less dray. One of the cubs
gazed at the train and seemed to meet my eyes,
reminding me of Russell. Not much else
to see, except the antelope, which flock to steam and iron
like it was mother. In just six months, you'll hug me
but never that $500. Best to Todd and Russell.
Your loving husband ($9.50 poorer),
                             Averill.

Furnace

I think of it as a lake
of yellow steel breaking the darkness—
almost spectral, sizzling with waves
that bake your skin. I toss in
fist-sized rocks of iron,
manganese, and chrome
and shut the door on the light.

Night shift passes like a drunk.
A man hoists trays of heavy molds
onto a shelf and groans. A spotter
pushes a giant magnet through the air
and signals the crane man, just so,
to release a ton of steel
upon two skinny rails
that bend, then hold. The spotter wails
in celebration or in curse—who knows?—
into the midnight caverns of the plant.
I watch the slinger crew conclude
its awkward dance. Low-man cleans up.
He pushes the leftover sand into piles
then through a pit on to a ceaseless belt.

Too tired to make small talk,
my partner tells me how two young guys died—
brothers, they were pouring on the wheel,
when one guy dropped his ladle
on the ground below. He passed out
from the heat into the ankle-deep spill.

His brother stepped in, started to go down. . .
My partner's voice trails off
in the fluorescent buzz of the lunchroom,
but I see them, two boys splashing
in a pond of yellow steel
until the wheel crew pulls them out.
The burn unit wrapped them in someone else's skin

for two days, when their lungs gave out.

All men look like devils
in the furnace light. The furnace tender
was a sorcerer as well
with me as his apprentice, stumbling
around the ten-ton room that holds the light.

I don't remember the sorcerer's name
but he left the Pima reservation
when the mines shut down, and loved to play softball
even in a Phoenix summer. He nails a short branch
on the twenty-foot trunk of tree and gestures
for me to take hold of it. "There isn't much
to slagging a furnace. . . Be careful."

And then the door opens,
and the lake seems to lean toward me
bright yellow in the visor-green.

I run the tree into the glowing center
and skim the golden coals of slag
from the sizzling waves, back and forth,
like raking a lawn. "Good enough!"
my partner hits my shoulder, "Come on!"

Once in the parking lot, we wake up
from the nightmare-hours to the red sun
rising through palm trees in a little park.
A thin mist wreathes the paddle boats
and the shabby dock of the duck pond.
Behind us, the foundry smokes and shrieks.

We slump over our beers, gray as ghosts,
and wonder where we'll be next year.
Most will get better jobs, and some (like me)
get hurt. But if you're tough enough to stick it out
you'll get laid off when the plant shuts down.
We see the future, each and every ghost.

Then I drive home, up Baseline Avenue,
past the Japanese flower farms
crowding the new air with acres of petals.

I try to shut the light out of the house
and pull the sheets over my skin,
glad that it's cool enough to sleep.
I think about a tree, the tamarack,
that never burns.

I skim it over sizzling waves
and reach into the lake of yellow steel.
Hours later, the afternoon light
splashes me awake.

Guadalupe AZ

Houses, without much house, with a postage stamp
of sand for a lawn, a wrecked cactus, and a toddler
who screws up her face, her black eyes following
everyone. Beside her, a bike with a twisted frame,
no tires or seat, a spare parts
inheritance, a rusting in desert brilliance.

The Res—humming to life, as someone plays
Freddy Fender and the Texas Tornadoes
through a glass door, not broken. Noon,
and the sun is too hot, even for devils.
At the taco stand, I eat nopalitos with Ray
from the foundry. We work in that hell-hole,

balancing on a ten-ton furnace, twisting
carbon electrodes, hand grinding steel,
tapping out molds with a five-foot bar. That afternoon,
a wear plate crushes my foot, five-hundred pounds.
I can see a line of palms in the distance, wavering
in the smog of Phoenix. I can see it clearly

as I stagger to get someone's help. The whole night long,
after the Demerol wears off, I hear: *I saw you
crying* and worship, in my own *chapel*, our children
and their children, in all the Ibuprophen towns.
Three months later—a swamp cooler
drips in the blazing alley, and I walk on my one good foot

with children too wise to cry.

Furnace Tenders at Dawn

He slumps on a pile of scrap—his wrinkles
glowing pink through a varnish of black sweat—
and pitches one shoulder against the scorched wall, as if
he were holding and being held up. The air breaks open—
sun spreads through the dust. His partner walks out
and hears the older man's breath, the sifting sound
of air in charred lungs, and drops his hands,
carbon-black, to a spot on the older man's back.
His thumbs press circles beside the neck
as he works at the muscles, as if they were machines
that needed shut down at the end of the shift. The hands
work the fiery demons out, the shift after shift,
the rumble of the furnace, the jab of the oxygen lance,
the blast, and the baking heat on his skin
as he opens the door on the yellow-white steel—
and it grips him again in that fiery room. It's as if
he were that boy, thirty-years ago, who felt so unfit
for the work he's done ever since. The hands,
working overtime now, push the demons out—
the chrome, the iron, the heat after heat—
and the muscles relax. And the muscles relax
like machines that were hard to shut down
at the end of the shift. There's a joke, a gesture,
and both of them laugh. They toss
lunch boxes into their cars and drive off.

When I Was a Thing

We cleaned all week, hosed load-outs,
swept the main floors where the tour
would come through, and painted railings,
painted yellow lines over everything,
even the dirt that was baked in,
even the tailings and balling floor mud.
We painted neat lines—for the people
from Pittsburgh would arrive at 11
with the new superintendent, and they cared
for the neatness of painted lines.

They came through the pellet plant
wearing spotless hard hats and dressed
like they were going out to the country club
for drinks and golf. I sat on a fork truck
stacking rollers, as one of them
caught my eye. And there I sat, a *thing*—
in the din of grinding and turning parts—
as he walked by. And I laughed to myself
at the secret, which he'd never know:
"There is a human being inside."

Summer Words

on the Iron Range, with Plutarch, a co-worker, and Bob Dylan

The first time I got laid off
from U.S. Steel, I went into the woods
with Brian, who had a chain saw
and a couple of acres of spruce to stump.
Each morning he pulled up in his Monte Carlo,
which he could no longer pay for, and I hopped in
with my thermos. Brian gunned it
and we slid over the icy ruts of town
into the woods. It was like entering the mines
on day-shift, but instead of the mills
banked nine stories high—the towering trees!

Brian's saw worked a wedge on one side
and then he pushed the great trunk from the other
until a hundred feet of spruce
balanced above us, looked down. Soon it would crash
and I'd start limbing—the branches
exploding like crystal in the surly air.

We'd pile a couple of stacks and take a break
to pull our sweat shirts off, soaked through
from the work. In Northern Minnesota
the work will get you quicker than the cold
which is, as Plutarch said, so serious
that words congeal as soon as they are spoken.
Those are the kind of words we shared
on the Iron Range. Frozen words.
We burned a cigarette and watched the mist
curl from a fist-sized thermos cup.

**

After my second layoff, I got a job
stitching hospital pads for minimum wage.
An old timer saw me walking through the town

40

I lived in, and his jaw dropped
at the sight of a lunch pail.
"Oh, you got a job—that's good!"

**

In *North Country Blues,* Bob Dylan sings about
the red ore mines shutting down. When I got there
the ore was gray, called taconite, but at one time
dirt and dust were red
and smelled of the blood of immigrant miners.

**

Brian sold the wood we cut, joined the National Guard,
and drank a lot.
One day he came to the bar I used to frequent
and we talked—not the hard words,
the frozen words that he'd grown up with,
but the words that Plutarch meant
when he said one day they would thaw out
and become the words you need.
For hours, we spoke those summer words.

Never Leaving Duluth

Riding northeast, I enter the city from a glacial hill,
crushed into a lip—from which block after city block
descend, in breathtaking steps, a ladder
reaching into an ocean of lake—I almost expect
the houses to fall into the lead-colored sea, which is always
too cold to swim in, too huge to freeze.

In the center, in the very depths of town,
a commerce of orange cranes feeds the last
of the brittle ships with marbles of iron. Soon,
the port will close due to winter storms.

Night comes on, night of cabbies and all-night drivers,
of plowmen in rubber packs, who stamp their feet
in the warmth of a diner, find a place at the counter, tell
    sly jokes.

I walk down the sidewalk, and sheets of plastic—
stretched and stapled against the wind—deaden the
    late-night news.
Old people argue—not making a sound. And then I see them
near the wall of a gutted house in the hueless night—
he holds an amber bottle and pulls it away
from a woman, who reaches for it three times,
till he hugs her and gives her a swig.
She throws back her head, and laughter rings out,
a laughter both hot and cold, sweet and mean.

The first settlers to Duluth, according to legend,
were welcomed by the Lakota people, overstayed,
and couldn't afford to leave. Now, we stare at the city,
terraced in circles above us, drink brandy all night
    in frozen parkas,
speak in a language both sweet and mean.

Wyoming

Just off Route 80, the dust
from the high plains is furious.
Even the antelope sway uneasily.
I spot a van in a cracked creek bed,
sheep huddled around it, backside to face.
Wind stings my eyes as I open the window
and hear country music, with flutes,
flooding the prairie with high notes,
surprising me in this iron land.

A shepherd leaps from the van—"Amigo!"—
he calls. He's leather-faced, wiry,
like the grass that whips around fence rails.
He offers a beer, as if he'd expected me
and had grown thirsty waiting. He searches
for words, for the right signal, and says—
"I learned English in Lima."

As we sit on the tailgate,
hunching our heads to keep out the wind,
his dog sidles up, short-legged and scruffy.
"I hunt rabbits—" he points at the rifle,
which he keeps ready, on a box of canned beans—
"Everything else is the same as my country.
Here, I live in a van and guard sheep,
but all lands are the same. We have war—
we have the same wind."
 He offers another beer, but I have to go.
"I drive this way often," I try to assure him—
"to visit Green River—"

He searches my eyes, waves after me
in my rear view mirror, climbs back in his van.
Along the state road, I spot some spring flowers
trying to bloom and hear the flutes,
rising over the plains, over the wind,
all the way to Route 80.

Magnesium

for John Langford

More than a metal,
mag comes from ponds near the Great Salt Lake
and brews in a ramshackle factory
prickling with magnetism and brown with rust.

We cast mag into ingots slippery as brine
and grab them with steel handles.
We stack ingots until our coveralls
are caked with salt—so we can make

mag cheap enough for pop tabs
and racing wheels. Shift after shift
Mag sucks its value from us,
but we are the ones transformed.

More than a metal, we cast these ingots
from a rage of lightning.

American Poem

I have studied the history of America.
I have gone to bars and gotten crazy
in towns that no longer exist
from the Chesapeake to the red Mesabi.

I saw the witch-hunt rise and fall
like profit-taking on the Dow.
I saw the Great Lakes from a grain elevator
and My Lai in the newspapers.

I drank moonshine in West Virginia
and watched Baghdad on television.
I slept in the valley of the only river
flowing north. And what do I think

of this America? As Chief Black Hawk said:
"Nesso Chemokemmon—Nesso Chemokemmon."

Blue Grass Poem

You were spilling your guts out, as usual,
as we drove into the Blue Grass State
from the West Virginia side, looking for work.
We wanted to pick up on the rumors,

so we stopped for some fast food,
and they told us one steel mill was running
but the other one was down, and a lot
of folks would have trouble this Christmas.

I checked the want ads while you talked,
and then we went back through the parking lot,
hands in pockets, shoulders bumping, you talking,
and the traffic fell on your voice like earth.

I could see what you were saying, only too late.
And then we left the Blue Grass State.

At Hawks Nest, West Virginia

Little known today, the building of the Hawks Nest Tunnel
by Union Carbide in 1930-31 claimed the lives of at least
800 men—to silicosis, many within months.

The steep mountains, like loaves of bread,
rise over the river at nightfall. Black laborers
camp out on the hillside, joking:
"Don't fall asleep, now,
you'll roll into the river."

They came from all over the South
to work in the Hawks Nest tunnel.
They drilled through a mountain of glass
without water to hold down the dust.
Gang after gang went off to the face

with handkerchiefs over their mouths.
One doctor did an autopsy on a man
and broke his knife on the lungs.
They knew rage—rage and the fear
of gasping for breath that's not there.

The last ones alive heard the river break through
and fell back, amazed, at what their black arms—
at the terrible work they could do.
Climb down to the river at nightfall.
Put your ear to the Hawks Nest tunnel.

Coming Home from Hoot-Owl Shift

As I walk past the scrapped-out furnaces,
pigeons flap and coo like the second coming,
and I think about why coal miners
always say hoot-owl, not grave-yard.

I scrape the ice from my car
and sniff the air—too cold and clear
for my sooty lungs—and drive home some twenty miles
past the mines—Monongah,
Farmington—forgotten mass graves.

And the dog-holes—
too many to name
in towns like Dellslow and Rivesville.

The sharp light of the sun
fills my windshield
from a line of mountains. At the edge,
I catch the ribbed whiteness
of frail-looking goats, heads down
in somebody's lawn.

Decker Creek spills over, chilling every gray stone.

I drive through Saberton
to the top of our mountain. From here I can see
the empty lot of Sterling Faucet
and a supermarket. I can almost read
how much chili costs
and if they're hiring.

—You remember
how that winter in West Virginia
someone smelling of shampoo
pulled the covers back
and drew the warmth from your sleeping body
into his freezing hand?

Lou Gehrig at the MDA Clinic in Morgantown WV

As I enter the waiting room
I see a life-size poster of the iron man.
He's more handsome than Gary Cooper
as he leans on his bat—the knob
pressed into the heel of his hand—
and he is not even thinking that
the round end in the turf
could wander out from under him.
(Oh, how the fit
relax in such awkward positions,
how a schoolgirl can sit
cross-legged on the hard floor
for hours, as if she were Gandhi;
how a boy can hang off a couch
watching TV upside down
and not even notice it.) And there is not
the slightest suggestion of a crutch
in the way he leans on the bat.

The other patients in the waiting room
browse *Family Circle*, or their own thoughts,
as if it were their job—even the children,
whose wisdom is like a desert island
(quietly, they assert their existence
although they might never be discovered).

Lou does not connect with them
because he has the eyes of a hero,
limpid, prepared for anything
but this. I try to comfort the iron man
in the poster, but it isn't necessary.
He is still leaning on his bat,
years from discovering
the disease that will bear his name.

Monongah WV

On December 6, 1907, the Fairmont Coal Co. exploded,
killing all of the miners on day shift. The official count
of 360 overlooked many immigrants.

1.

Every December 6, I drive to this place
along Route 19, near the banks of the Tygart,
and turn my car toward the wrinkled flow
of the West Fork River, and stop. The fresh snow
crests around rocks and debris.
In the water, old antifreeze bottles knock
against each other, like aimless chimes.

2.

A spark ignites Fire Damp, the methane blows,
flames rush from speck to speck—like the breath
of a surging dragon, licking the coal dust
suspended in haulageways, spitting fire,
reaving stout timbers, seeking, by instinct,
live bones among fossils, devouring the faces
before they can scream, as the men duck,
are sucked into blazing entries or crouch
in a shelter of ash, by crimson steel cars.

3.

I'm in a meadow
filled with the threadbare gray
of five hundred women in the snow. They sob
to the heavens, gaunt as the heavens are
in West Virginia. I ask them to leave,
for we're in danger from another explosion,
but the women won't go. Eyes starving
for news, they peer from snow-soaked scarves,
babushkas, chadors, prayer shawls.

The mine blows again, and the earth trembles
like the hide of a frightened mule.

4.

I blink and the West Fork River
seems to sizzle beneath the snow's touch.
The fog drifts off down the river,
between two banks of melting snow,
toward Morgantown and Pittsburgh,
cities of what once was—

the smoke and fire
in the human heart.

5.

This spring, I'll drive out to this place,
this wilderness between rivers.
The meadow will fill with survivors, and
five-hundred threadbare women
will clutch their dusty lovers and go home.

The Seventy-Ninth Miner

November 19, 1968

He could have been the seventy-ninth.
It was his first job, and he couldn't sleep.
After the moon rose, he stared through the window
into the backyard, which he'd just mowed, to the
creek, overgrown with sumacs and maples.

He heard the tires slick by in the rain,
walked past his parents' door, and listened
to the sound his father made, the breathing.
His father worked daylights at the face
but already he couldn't sleep lying down.

His mother looked tired in the kitchen light
from the dust—but more from contending
with everything else. "Your bucket's ready.
Eat something." He looked into his hands
and then the boy spoke: "I could get a job

in the glass plant or the carbon factory."
More hoot-owl traffic went by in the rain
and one of the cars pulled into the drive.
For a moment, she stared at her son
as if she were giving him a bath and needed

to study his body for cuts or bruises.
Then she got up, breaking the watch,
and waved the car on. It sped off, late now,
for hoot-owl shift at Consol Number Nine.
Five months later, the mine kept exploding

even after they sealed the portal with concrete
and steel—on the other seventy-eight.

The Machinist and the Cell Phone

Entering the machine shop was not like entering hell
or a prison—more like a night without sleep,
a few hand-cuts and metal splinters, a cold wind
under the steel roof with its I-beams and angle rafters,
the smell of the coolant, and the sound
of compressed air whistling in tapped holes
all midnight shift. And then there was Harry,
who ran the horizontal mills, his bald head
gleaming like milled aluminum, his face bright
from grandstanding beside his machine and telling stupid
    jokes
we had to laugh at—he was part of the sentence.

One shift I saw a phone in Harry's box, a cell phone,
beside the mics and dial calipers, which he kept safe,
like jewelry, on green felt. The phone lit up like an icon
waiting to be clicked, so I said: "Harry, what's a machinist
doing with a cell phone in his box—is it
for dealing drugs or trading stocks?" I pushed
my face into his. My words gleamed like a ground tool
between us. His face dulled as he told me
his son would be out plowing snow
from the county roads all night. "That leaves his mother
alone, and she has cancer. . . She might need someone
to talk her through the pain."

The mills howled, putting their fearful shine on everything.
I don't remember what I said, but Harry said, "That's o.k."
I sat down to a bin of parts that needed deburring,
    feeling like a prisoner
who wanted himself—more than his sentence—to disappear.

Even before I heard the ring, Harry was reaching
into his box, saying into his phone: "I'm here."

Every Cab Driver Has a Story

Imagine you're leaving a stylish tavern
in a Russian novel, past midnight,
with a sleepy fare in the back of your cab.
The snow on the streets of St. Petersburg
drifts axle-deep. You can tell it's by Gogol—

this novel you've been imagining—
for the smell of ammonia permeates
everything, irritating your eyes
like the icy wind or the frigid looks
of certain officials. When a storm like this

descends from the peaks of this rugged land
everyone needs your fishtailing cab.
You stare into the white-out of the window
and glance at your fare in the mirror, as if
you feared him more than the storm. He wears

a goatee—one so scruffy that only
the rich could get away with it—and cleans
his glasses with a handkerchief large enough
to sleep under. The gesture of cleaning
symbolizes the newly rich and their

obsession with newness. Then the new man
stares at your name on the taxi license
and repeats it—your foreign-sounding name.
The chill of this moment is hard to translate
from the Russian, but it's like a wall

of ice that you can't get over. The new man
wipes his glasses, as if he were the one
who had to see in this storm. And you feel
vulnerable, for you have a story—
every cab driver in this city has a story—

and the new man has none.

He's rubbing his glasses as the snow
buries the streets of St. Petersburg,
and you, the cab driver in this sudden storm,
drive through the turning pages, not blinking.

A Gin-Drinking Day

for Barbara

A lousy day, a gin-drinking day, with clouds
the color of wet cement. The creek
fills with muddy runoff, and a brown flood

rinses the bottomland, covers the ball field
and picnic grounds. The rolling river
washes the bass and trout downstream.

I stare through the window of my van
at a mountain with dark blue trees
slanting into the icy rain—each cold leaf,

each thin stem, bends in the downpour—
weak but supple, like the wrist
sustaining a child's palm. Arriving home,

I wait for you and mix two gin and tonics,
while darkness brims with the sound of ice
and mixes with a drum-roll of rain.

Two Girls, Fishing

for Lily and Adelheid

Headsets in dyed hair,
nodding to music,
lip-synching,
they pause only to hook their worms
and cast, medium length,
to a spot near a sunken raft
into the cooler water
where bass and trout are feeding.

On a Triumph 650

She expected nothing from the relationship
but a Ford Galaxie and a sunny day to wax it in.

He backed into the thing, only afterward realizing
he was looking for whatever would cut him loose

from nomad friends—while she was content with a cooler
    full of Michelob
and a bowl of Cheetos, never dreaming of a man

whose every wish was a roll of the dice. She was looking
for a solid body to make her forget

one of the worst hangovers in the West. They skirted about,
with an absence of art that was almost grace and one day met

in a working class district that had not been gentrified,
whose brick walls, scorched by the stories of thousands,

offered a screen while they undressed. At last, they were
    content
to get drunk and live forever. Their beings dissolved and
    merged

so many times the he-want/she-want
of it was lost, but not on them. They disappeared into Arizona,

stepping beyond categories, into real life
and out, splitting the air on a Triumph 650.

Part II. *In Dade Coal Mine*

In Dade Coal Mine

Letters and prison fragments

+

FROM THE TRIAL RECORD

"I guess you didn't know
this here was stolen goods,"
the deputy said, to which
Lancaster responded:
"It wasn't stolen,
it was the watch
my master gave me—
Martin LeConte,
the famous scientist—
because it didn't work.
Here, Lancaster, he said,
If anyone can fix it,
I guess you can."

+

FROM THE PRISON LOG

LeConte, Lancaster. Age, 62.
Height, 5'9". Weight, 141 lb.
nativity, South Carolina.
Complexion, mulatto. Hair,
black. Eyes, brown. Scar,
right shoulder and right
side of face. Scars from
whipping, buttocks
and back. Sentenced
in Liberty County,
state of Georgia. Date,
May 22, 1887.
Term, 3 years. Crime,
receiving stolen goods.
To be served at Rising Fawn
convict labor camp
for work in Dade coal mine.

+

LETTER I

TO: Master Martin LeConte, Northern California
FROM: Lancaster LeConte, Rising Fawn Labor Camp

Dear Master, if anyone can fix this situation,
I guess you can. I only hope you're so inclined.
I'm asking you, in your own hand, to witness
that the watch was given not stolen.

Also, legal help of $65.
Without it, they won't review the evidence.
I do not put a price on years of service—
although they weren't freely given—
but does that mean there is no debt?
At least honor the debt to yourself
as a scientist, to be true and witness
the truth about the gift of the watch.

It's June. This plea will reach you
in California in a few weeks time.
I might be still alive at Rising Fawn.
Yesterday, I saw a man chained to his bunk
while a rat crept from the straw
and ate the food from his plate.
He didn't move. For all I know,
the man was dead. What could I do
for him?—Or any of us do?

These men are without help,
but I have you. You can help
by telling the simple truth
about the gift of a watch—
a watch that didn't work.

+

LETTER II

TO: Master Martin LeConte, Northern California
FROM: Lancaster LeConte, Rising Fawn Labor Camp

Dear Master,
do you remember
when I helped you
in your lawn, observing
"vertical rays
from a luminous source"—
the streamers touched your lawn
from the very heavens. Yes,
you were making observations,
concerning the effect
of light upon the eye
and as you spoke to yourself,
you awakened something,
a seeing both
of wonder and understanding.
I thank you, although perhaps
it wasn't your intention.

"Star rays—" you said—
"produced by a refraction
of light upon a lawn in Georgia."

+

LETTER III

TO: Master Martin LeConte, Northern California
FROM: Lancaster LeConte, Rising Fawn Labor Camp

The owner of the mine, about my age—
years ago, he was a guest at your plantation.
I recognized him, yesterday, when he came to the mine.
He has a politician's smile. That's how I knew him.

Old Henry says he rents us from the state of Georgia
for $10 a year. His name—Gov. Joseph Brown.
I hope your study progresses—
into the nature of things.

+

LETTER IV

TO: Master Martin LeConte, Northern California
FROM: Lancaster LeConte, Rising Fawn Labor Camp

Let me ask you, Master, where do you get your heat?
Even in Northern California, it must get cold in winter.
Do you go out and saw the wood?

The trees out there—Redwoods, Pines, Sequoias—
they are gloriously high—
must take eternity to saw.

Careful, now, you have to put a notch in one side,
and then somehow pull it down.
After that, comes limbing,

then saw the trunks to logs and split and stack them
beneath a sloped tin roof.
Then, and only then, the wood is fuel.

Maybe you get your heat from coal—if so, do you mine it?
Do you know what size of charge to set
and how to place it?

Master, this is something I've been learning. It is more
an art than science—and dangerous to learn.
There are no failing students in a mine.

Now, ply your scoop. Coal cars don't fill themselves.
Five minutes of this work,
and you're as Black as I am.

If there were any justice in the words we use,
I'd be the Master. In the Academy of Wood and Coal,
I've gone to school, earned an advanced degree—

Master of the Fine Art of providing fuel.
Have you attended such a hard and useful school?

+

LETTER V

TO: Master Martin LeConte, Northern California
FROM: Lancaster LeConte, Rising Fawn Labor Camp

Master, did you know Dr. Raines?
He's a man about my age.
Perhaps you knew him in his better years.
Today, he showed up drunk, stumbling at the shack
they call a hospital. Twelve men were lying there
on stretchers. The Doctor took another drink
and cocked his ear, as the Captain shouted—

"What do you see here, on these stretchers?"
"I see twelve fit men," the Doctor answered,
"laying-about, trying to get out of work."

"All of them?" Captain hollered out.
"Every mother's son," the Doctor chimed.
"Then certify them fit—I'll find trusties
to haul them back into the mine."

I lay there on my stretcher
because of rheumatism and a hacking cough,
waiting to be certified as fit by Dr. Raines,
that funny Doctor—who never cured a man,

but he could empty a hospital
by signing his name.

+

FRAGMENT I

1863. I slept by day, ran toward the coast by night,
coming near to a little cabin
where a woman slept on a broken-down porch
in the open air, because of the heat.

"Shh," I said. Her eyes went wide
as she awoke. "Tell me," I asked her,
"Where I can find the Colored Troops."

"That would be the island," she replied.
"I have a boat, and I can take you there."

I never went on such wide water.
She saw how nervous I became
and told the story, as she rowed,
of how she gained her freedom.

This is what we spoke of in those days,
the great promise. We rolled a little
in the waves. The moon shone on the tips of foam
and on the wide dark water.

+

FRAGMENT II

1865. We no longer fear our masters
for they have lost the war, and our freedom
is an everyday thing. We are not only soldiers
but saviors—bent on Reconstruction.

It was the rebel troops
who torched the port of Charleston
so our advancing colored regiments
couldn't shelter and provision ourselves
within the walls. The fire got into warehoused cotton
and raged as we approached. The mayor rode out
with a white flag in front and flames at his behind
in a panic to surrender to Col. Bennett.
"Help us!" He cried. We got the people out,
fought fire with what little water we could pump,
blew up infernos to slow the spread, and on the fourth day
of dancing in flames and sucking smoke—
the city was saved, what was left of it: charred walls
without roofs, burnt earth and stones, and some buildings,
including a waterfront district. Smoke and ash
floated in the air like autumn leaves. We went inside
an odd market and warehouse, whose hard dirt floor
was implanted with manacles and iron cages and a stage
made of oak, untouched by flames, where the auctioneer
must have called out the starting price and fanned
the craze for ownership. We walked around
and studied. For most of us,
it was our first museum,
and it was quiet.

+

FRAGMENT III

I did not get a penny for my 18 months of service
as a U.S. soldier, but in Oct. 1863
you received $300 compensation
from the U.S. government
for the loss of just one slave
named Lancaster.

After all these years of pain,
even as a dead man,
I will demand the part that's mine—

but you—
how would you even know
what part was yours
without the whip?

+

FRAGMENT IV

This is how they whet the whip.
First, the captain dumps a pail of water
in the red earth, passing the leather
between the sole of his boot
and the mud—all eight feet of it.
"This here's my negro negotiator,"
he says, as if he were explaining
something to a simple child.
He's said it a thousand times
and always with the same grin.
"I think that you'll agree with me,"
he whispers—"Just let me
explain the situation." He has
a friendly twinkle in his eyes
and goes on, speaking in an even,
confidential tone that no one else
can hear, except the convict
who is being whipped and the
convict next in line. Yesterday,
I heard him, every word.
I heard him twice.

+

FRAGMENT V

Today I heard a roof-fall, slate thudding deep
in Number Three. I was working on my side
in three-foot coal, trying to drive in timbers
with a five-pound hammer—the meat and sinew
throbbing in my arm. I rolled over on my back

to listen: *"Bring hoist and bars—*
he's still alive!" I couldn't see except for shadows,
but I heard men scramble to his rescue—
"Pry that rock, Thompson! Hey, McCutcheon,
get ready, you're gonna put a sling beneath—"

It was Old Henry—the man who'd taught me,
taught all the prisoners how to stay alive
in hell. He was taking charge in darkness,
until the Captain cut him off—*"Get back to work!"*—
The sound of picks and pry-bars paused

and then continued with their rescue-music.
From where I knelt, one knee in muck,
I glimpsed the Captain's lamp, light playing over stone,
as he made for the spot marked by the shadows
of the men, men straining, men leveraging the rock—

"Get back to work!" He boomed again, without effect.
Voices broke out, whoops and hollering,
which told me they were nearly through, had torn away
the rock-fall and could almost touch the man—
almost reach out and feel his hand. The touch of life

delivered back from death—that's what they felt,
or almost felt. And then a blast—expelling something—
the smoke invisible but not the blood, the heart-throb
coating the walls, drenching the coal-dust red
as it spurted from the belly of a man. I was on all fours

almost thirty yards away and heard the Captain growl
as if he were an animal, trained to order men—
"Now there's two dead niggers—one under those rocks
and Thompson, here. Who wants to be the third?"
From where I knelt, I couldn't see but knew

each face was set against the Captain—
eyes drawn to a slit, and every fist squeezed shut.
"I got Old Henry here!" the Captain said.
"Let it be me!" I heard Old Henry cry
and then a blast. I crept into the haulage-way

and saw the Captain kick a shape of shadow
that was Old Henry once. And then a voice—
"Let it be me!" I heard the voice rise up,
and it was mine, but not just mine—
our voices echoed through the earth, from every face

and entryway, until the Captain spoke—
"That man you're rescuing—you bring him out alive,
my rifle sends him straight to hell." Then silence,
which can last forever in a mine. It can defeat a man
or many men. I felt it then. And then I heard

the sound of men, of men who would be saviors
going back to work, back to our places at a face
shaped from a dark eternity of coal. A song
rose through the pit, curling around wedged timbers,
over narrow-gauge tracks, through rock falls

and coal-dust motes, through blasts and endless silences—

"Been working here, in Dade coal mine—
been working here.
I'm almost done my sentence
of life plus just one year."

+

FRAGMENT VI

One of the whipping bosses told me,
"A miner is like a bird," because
the labor of a skilled free man
is so much in demand

he can pick up and go—
for a free man to pick up and go—
for a miner to be like a bird—
here today and gone tomorrow!

If I were that bird, I'd fly
into the blue light of the sky.
Below me—rhododendron blooming
all over Raccoon Mountain.

I'd drift above the shaft hole,
coke ovens, convict shacks—
and then fly higher still,
high above the whipping post.

From such a height, I'd see
some years back to slavery
and far into the future, a hundred years,
when the miners will be like birds.

There won't be any prisoners, only birds.

+

AFTERWORD TO "IN DADE COAL MINE"

Lancaster LeConte died in Dade coal mine in 1889, after
having been certified fit for work by the state-apppointed physician,
Doctor Thomas Raines. Before that, he'd appealed to his former
master, Martin LeConte, requesting his testimony and $65 for legal
expenses. The prisoner never heard back. These are facts. Most of
the rest of this sequence is my invention. For the facts about convict
labor upon which this fiction is grounded, I am indebted to the
following scholars: Ronald L. Lewis, David Oshinsky, C.Vann
Woodward, Alex Lichtenstein, and Mathew Mancini.

The invented letters show Martin LeConte in a poor light. Is
this unfair? LeConte was not a reluctant slave-holder but an active
defender of slavery. In his sociological writings, he argued that, in
America as compared to past societies, "slavery had always been a
constituent and evolving element of a healthy civilization."
(LeConte, The Relation of Organic Science to Sociology, 58-59)
He attempted to buttress the slave-system's ideological position by
using his prestige in the world of science to say that "too rapid
change creates a fevered, unhealthy condition of the organism."
(same, p. 52) After the Civil War, LeConte fled the south for
California so as not to live under a Reconstruction government in
which free Blacks played an influential role.

I know nothing of the descendants of Martin LeConte. They
bear no responsibility for the sins of their progenitor. They have
nothing to apologize for, and this work has nothing to do with
them.

From Martin LeConte's own scientific articles, which he
published in *Science* magazine, I borrowed ideas for one of the
invented letters.

I accept responsibility for totally falsifying one fact. Lancaster
LeConte was not 62 at the time he was condemned to hard labor
but 75. To condemn a man of 75 to a sentence that amounted to
torture and death was an act of brutality beyond my power of
imagination—and impossible for many readers to accept, I
reasoned. So I made him younger, which didn't change the essence
of his story.

Thanks to giant labor and civil rights struggles, prison

conditions have changed greatly in the 117 years since the death of Lancaster LeConte. But forms of convict labor still exist, as does torture, which is practiced in prisons operated by the United States, at home and around the world. Capital punishment crowns this system, which houses fully one-quarter of the world's prison population. Now, as then, the United States should be classed as a jail-house nation.

This fictional sequence is my attempt to present Lancaster LeComte's appeal for justice. In honor of this convict laborer and former slave, I dedicate this work to the prison population in the United States today—a great portion of our humanity—unseen and unrecognized.

Part III. *John Henry's Partner Speaks*

John Henry's Partner Speaks

The following transcriptions are based on tapes of interviews
with Phil Henderson, close friend of John Henry, the legendary
steel-driver, known in myth as the man who died racing the steam
drill. The interviews were conducted in 1937-38 in Baltimore, when
Henderson was about 90 years old. How these tapes came into my
possession is a story that I am glad to tell, but on another occasion. I
attempted to publish the transcriptions in the form of articles, which
I sent to numerous American history and folklore journals, without
success. Then it occurred to me that with very few changes, the
tapes could be put into free verse, which might stand a better chance
of acceptance. Henderson spoke remarkably well for a man born in
slavery. The grammar and word choice needed little correction.
Insofar as the facts alluded to in these tapes could be checked, I have
done so, and will testify that all the historical particulars are
accurate. Except for headnotes and footnotes, what follows are the
words of John Henry's partner, Phil Henderson.

1. TWO SKINNY KIDS

You think that he sat on his father's knee
and told him, "Hammer be the death of me?"
He was born a slave—I know what he would have said:
"Papa, I'll be a free man some day."

But he never knew his mother or father.
He was raised by mine. I'll tell you
the real life of Phil and John.
It's not all racing a steam drill.

We were two skinny kids—when the Civil War started
we got better food, and John filled out. He was tall
for a slave, over six feet. White men would ask
where he got his strength, and John always said,

"I got it from Africa."

2. LOOKING FOR WORK

John and Phil have just left the property in Virginia where they'd been slaves to pursue jobs on the C & O Railroad. They arrive in Tazewell, June 28, 1867, in time for the hanging of the outlaw, Ben Hardin.

We left the hills and the river valley
where we'd been slaves, to look for work,
and followed the road into the mountains
where the air got thin and cold, though it
was June. Outside of Tazewell, a crowd—
mostly white, in their Sunday best,
had gathered in a field. Men lifted little boys
like there was a ball game or a revelation
to be witnessed. "They must have heard
we were coming," I said to John.
"The whole town turned out to greet us."
He pointed to a stepladder by a tree—"Or lynch us."

But it was Ben Hardin, the outlaw,
they meant to hang. He smoked a cigar
and leaned on the ladder, like he was the sham
of another man's hanging. He sang out,
in a voice like an auctioneer, the names
of the men he'd killed in Kentucky
before he came here to Tazwell,
where he'd killed a man for a horse.

He bragged that he'd shot them all in the back
and he'd do it again. Then he'd beg for mercy
and plead with the boys in the crowd—"Don't end up
like me at the end of a rope"—then clap his hands,
change his manner again, like a whirlwind
blowing this way and that.
                        Later I heard
how a teamster drove Ben from the jail
to the hanging tree. Ben laughed
at the worried teamster.—"No need to whip' em, son,
the show won't start till I get there."

Even when they fixed the black cap
so it covered his eyes, he never shut up.
He went up the ladder, jabbering every step,
until the sheriff hollered—"Kick!"—to his men,
and Ben crashed in the grass, because the rope,
not his neck, had snapped. —I'd say
somebody cut it part way through,
to worry the poor hung man, who moaned:
"Get me a doctor, my knees are broke."

His mood had turned, and no wonder,
from falling six feet in the dark of that cap
and expecting the rope to catch him
and lift him up into the dark
of another world, when it broke.

As the courier set off for the hardware store
to bring back a stronger rope, Ben roared:
"It ain't fair—to hang a man twice!"
This time, two men had to poke him
with their knives, drawing blood every step
of the way, as he backed up the ladder
to his perch. He was quiet now. The night
came on with a chill, which Ben must've felt
to his very bones. He turned his head
this way and that, like he was looking for mercy
somewhere in the dark of the cap. "Kick it again!"
the sheriff boomed out. The rope stretched
with Ben's weight, till it held with a crack—
like a shot in that thin mountain air.

I never knew a man's neck could make
such a sound. The last thing I remember
of poor Ben Hardin—he wore nice boots.
They kicked for a minute, like he thought
if he could recover his footing and climb
the thin air, one quick little step at a time,
he might still make it.
                              John Henry and me

were out of slavery less than a year. We'd seen
men whipped to death and beyond
but never seen anyone hung. "Come on!"
John said. "We need to get out of here."

3. THE ARMY

We left Tazewell and headed for Bluefield, WV,
where thousands of free men were shaping up
to work in the Great Bend Tunnel. They came
from Bland and Giles County, from Whythe,
Grayson, from as far away as Henry County,
and further than that. They walked by day,
stole food, and put down a bed roll
(if they had one) on the wet grass at night.
What an army—I thought, as we shaped up—
but where is our chief of staff? Our line
stretched as far as I could see, till we came
to a man hunched over a table. He asked:
"Can you do tunnel work?" and tossed out
the old or sick. Some of us wrote our names—
if we'd learned our letters, which John and I had—
most lived and died by an X.

4. BLIND AS TUNNEL MULES

When John and I showed up at the tunnel
we didn't know much, but we were smart enough
not to ask. After three weeks—

we walked out from night shift
blind as tunnel mules in the sun.
I followed John off the road to a holler,
filled with stones and dried muck
from the heading. I heard them
and then saw the men filling in,
their white skin shining. We were
so close I could hear their breath
and smell their sweat as they pulled
their rakes slowly, like they were counting
each solemn stroke on the unmarked earth.
A cloud of gray dust surrounded them
as they raked small rocks in a mound—
that place was the colored burying ground.

"Start walking," John told me,
and we went back the way we came
like it was a picnic we weren't invited to
and had to get home.

5. IN THE DUST OF THE GREAT BEND TUNNEL

Work can be sweet, I guess,
but I worked for the C & O Railroad
up by the face of that hard, red shale,
spitting out dust, wiping splinters of rock
from my nose and mouth.

—Are you there, Philip?
John's voice would ring out.
I was an arm's length away turning steel.
I turned it and gave it a shake
to let the loose rock fall out.
When I was ready I'd answer back
—Can you drive her, HUNH?
And John would sing out
—I can drive her, HUNH!
And every time he said *HUNH!*
his hammer struck steel.

Then he'd sing a line
—This hammer gonna be the death of me—
to give me a chance to turn steel and give it a shake
in the hole, and we'd start over.

—Can you sing, Philip, can you sing?
—I can sing, John, can't you hear me sing?
*—I can sing, HUNH!—*and the hammer rang out.

We sang
and the hammer would have the last word.

6. THE DEATH OF RUSSELL MATHENY

—Don't slip, Philip,
—Watch your own step, John.
—Gettin' ready, wipin' sweat off my brow,
—Don't fall out brother I need you now.

Russell was one of a few white men
who worked with us at the face.
The rock floor we worked on
was full of lard-oil and black strap
from the machines and the lamps.
One night he slipped at the wrong time.

When the water-boy came by, we'd take a break.
After Russell died, they gave us a liquor break.
You think I'm joking but it happened
after a good fellow died at the face.
Here's a little drop to keep your minds
on the job, the boss might say. We knew
what that meant. Drink and forget.
Feel that liquor burn and forget.
We felt that liquor burn but we didn't forget.

—This whiskey ain't free,
  Russell Matheny paid for every drop.
—Some day the whiskey's gonna be on me.

7. GOING HOME

Phil gets word that his father is ill and knows that, by the time the message arrived, the old man was probably dead. The next day John presents Phil $20 raised from the men for his journey home.

On my way home, I rode in the wagon
owned by a man and woman, whose skin
was a shade lighter than their mules.
I thanked them for going out of their way
to take me to the bottomland
of the river, where my parents lived.

Mom showed me his grave, still muddy,
on the steep hillside by a colored church.
"We're just getting started," the preacher said.
He gestured at the wet earth,
his hand waving over only three graves.
One was a kin of mine, twenty years old,
killed by a white man. The other plot
held a child and mother, sharing one grave—
they were killed by a different kind of anger.
The third was my father's muddy grave.
"Don't be in such a hurry
to fill that yard," I told the preacher.

I gave Mom the $20 and said:
"Find a stone that he'd have liked—
spend the rest on food and clothes."
She stared, along with my sisters and a nephew,
because not one of the Henderson family
ever had a real stone, let alone bought clothes.

They thought I'd made a man of myself
in the white man's world, so I told them
I couldn't afford that stone, but I was rich
from the friendship of John and the tunnel men.
I described what a worker John was. No harm
could come to me since he was my friend.

Two days later, I caught another cart,
bouncing ruts for a day and a half, to return
to the camp of the Great Bend Tunnel.

My family, my neighbors, and a few folks
I hardly knew, waved goodbye to me.
And my father was there, on fire with life,
standing beside the house, looking strong
as the last time I saw him alive
when he drove me off. He was angry,
waving his hands as if he meant to stir a wind
that would drive me off again. He cursed me
in his great voice, which no one but me could hear.
Then he waved, and I waved back. Thank you,
I thought, for teaching me how to hold spikes
without flinching, make a bed roll, and cover
my tracks. And thank you for driving me off.

The cart hit all the ruts, but somehow
I protected the pie my mother sent
with instructions for John not to share.
Those were orders John never got to keep.

At the point when Phil arrives back at the Great Bend Tunnel,
the tape becomes increasingly difficult to transcribe, because he is
obviously upset by the story he has to tell. I played this part of the
tape over and over, until I was afraid the tape would wear thin and
break between reels. Each time I heard it, I imagined Phil
Henderson, this fine old man, sitting beside me in the darkness, his
usually strong voice breaking down.

The sorrow that broke Phil's voice stemmed from the tragedy he
discovered on his return to the tunnel camp. The first fact,
communicated to him by Polly, Phil's friend and John's intimate
companion, was that John Henry was dead, murdered at the behest
of C & O Railroad.

Developments at the camp had come to a head while Phil was
gone, including the Railroad's threat to lay off night shift due to the

91

supposed efficiency of the steam drill. Apparently, Phil and John knew all about the steam drill—they'd operated it themselves on numerous occasions. It was efficient chiefly because of their skill as operators.

To forestall this layoff, and for no other reason, John challenged the steam drill to a race, which he easily won. This event has been made famous, in a greatly distorted form, in the folk song, which the reader is doubtless familiar with.

After winning the race, John called a gathering of all the tunnel workers from all shifts, Black and white (Irish is the term Phil uses), to discuss the layoff, which was still rumored. That was on Thursday. The following Saturday John was found at the bottom of a holler (near the burial ground referred to in part 4 of this work) with his head broken in and a bottle of whiskey, unbroken, in his right hand.

But John was never a heavy drinker, Polly pointed out. And if he were drunk enough to fall and break his head, would he have had the wherewithal to clutch his bottle and defend it from breaking all the way to the ground? Along with these valid objections, Phil raised that when John did drink whiskey, he always held the bottle in his left hand, because he carried a sharpened piece of steel (a rude knife) in his belt, so that he could easily grab it with his stronger right hand. This was a 'whiskey-drinking' precaution that Phil's father had taught the two of them.

According to Polly, the tunnel workers knew exactly what happened. The Railroad had permitted several outlaw gangs to operate in the vicinity of the tunnel-camps. The words ruffians, bullies, or thugs are too kind a description. They were one reason why the C & O had a captive workforce, for if a tunnel worker were foolish enough to quit, the poor man might well be found after his last payday on one of the trails leading away from camp, murdered and stripped of his last week's pay.

At this point in the story, a blacksmith whom Phil refused to name, so many years later, brings two horses to Polly and Phil. On first seeing the horses, Phil is dazzled by them and can only think of what fine animals they are, marveling at how "their withers shone like two hillsides beneath a full moon."

The sight of this white man leading two fine horses may have surprised Phil, but Polly knew what these horses were for. Closely identified with John Henry, his two best friends were now in danger from the gang that had killed John. Polly had made arrangements with this sympathetic blacksmith, who remains anonymous to us and was, we can only hope, unknown to the vengeance of the railroad gangs. The two fugitives had to lead, push, and pull their mounts several miles through the near-jungle brush of West Virginia.

8. ESCAPE ON THE GREENBRIER RIVER ROAD

Through sassafras and fronds of sumac, we pushed our
      horses.
Just before dawn, we found the trail, high above the
      Greenbrier,
and urged our horses on, daring to hope for the first time,
now, we could get free of the railroad gangs.

Our horses made time for a few good miles,
till we rounded a bend and ran into a wall of man-sized
      boulders
blocking the road. We looked for a path around
but ended up down at the river, again—

            urging our mounts into the water,
            trying to stay on the sandy shoals—
            but the bottom dropped off more than once
            and we plunged in—our horses
            up to the withers in white water—
            before we hit sand or mud again.

That afternoon, I started a fire because we were soaked to the
      skin
and tired. Polly pulled off her shift and placed it on a hickory
      branch
and asked me to leave her alone. I put my things by hers and
      went off
in the woods to sleep, while our clothes dried by the fire till
      night.

On our second day, we saw the smoke of the west-shaft camp
and skirted it wide, and rode hard till we knew we were safe.
That night, we built our second fire and slept
while the river rolled far below, through rapids and shoals.

I woke up and thought of John—my partner, my friend.
Because of the strength in his body—and something even
      stronger

than muscles that was in him—he was an older brother to me—
now gone. The fire had burned down to coals, and the dew
  came on.

I tossed in the cold till the sound of the Greenbrier River
lifted me up and floated me off to sleep. When I woke up
  again,
Polly was breathing beside me, and I knew
we had strength between us to make up for John.

9. QUINNIMONT

The two fugitives have been following the Greenbrier River,
which empties into the New River (paradoxically, the New River
is the oldest river in North America and possibly the world).

High above the New River Valley, all we could see
was what seemed like a little stream,
half a mile straight down. It's a good thing
we could trust our horses—we were too dizzy
from hunger to care how close we got to the edge.
But those horses cared! We were about to give up
when we came to a sign that said *QUINNIMONT*—
Property NEW RIVER COAL CO. J. Beury, Owner.
We had been looking for civilization when we came
to Quinnimont, and could've done worse. The horses
were sold for a meal and first week's rent. And then
I sold myself to a fellow who needed to put in a shaft—
"Starting next year, we can sell all the coal we can mine,"
he said "—thanks to the C & O and that tunnel
they've drilled through the Great Bend Mountain."

That's when I first mined coal, and I've been
underground ever since—

10. THE GRAND TUNNEL BALL

Phil and Polly have moved up the New to the Kanawha River and the coal fields in Kanawha County. The ball referred to took place Feb. 15, 1873

They held a ball in White Sulphur Springs
to celebrate the commencement of the C & O line
carrying coal through the longest tunnel in North America,
at least to that date. They danced on a balcony over the river
and sipped champagne as they promenaded through a garden
of Japanese maples and giant hostas, while fifty wood stoves
kept them warm, so they could pause and admire
the Greenbrier River, which seemed to cascade
beneath their very feet. I remember that February.
Poly and I had moved to Kanawha County,
to a leaky cabin. We had some love between us,
a great deal, but it was a miserable cold February
without those fifty stoves to keep us warm.

I went downtown to check my mail
but never received an invitation to the ball.
In fact, none of the tunnel workers were invited.
No one who swung a hammer or turned steel—not one single
mucker or blaster or tool boy or sharpener. Not a blacksmith
or water boy, either. Not being there, how could we
congratulate ourselves on a job well done?
How could we beg to differ or comment on something
one of those silver-tongues had left out?
But what could a tunnel worker have said
that the world's great orators might have forgotten?

I might have mentioned the three hundred men
who died in the tunnel, so this ball could take place.

11. NO BLOOD ON ITS HANDS

Of course, the C & O had no blood on its hands.
Not the blood of anyone named McKnight,
Burl, or Anderson—no Johnson, no two men
named Robinson, no Roberts, not one each
of Turner or Holly—no three John Browns.*
No Underwood, Webster, Massey, or Moss—
not the white men, Lyttle, O'Megan,
Kennedy, Reilly, and two named Flynn—
not to mention Russell Matheny.

There were four men named Henry,
three of them John, but only one of them
was Phil Henderson's partner, John.

But the C & O had no blood on its hands
because the east tunnel was all contracted out
and the bills charged to W.R. Johnson, Co.

*John Brown was a name taken by many freed slaves. It was later
a popular given name, as in John Brown Henderson, Phil's oldest
son. His second son was also John, although he was called by his
middle name, Henry.

12. NO WINTER HEAT

Phil worked in West Virginia coal mines for many years. Near the end of his mining career, he was chosen to serve on the rescue team from his mine in Marion County, the first Black man to be so honored. After the Monongah disaster of 1907, the aging Phil seems to have ended his mining career and moved to Baltimore. He concluded his working life at the Bethlehem steel mill at Sparrow's Point and, finally, as building maintenance man in a tenement on the west side of Baltimore.

I never served in a war—
I served in the Great Bend Tunnel,
and worked in coal mines the rest of my life.
I saw as many men die as a soldier might,
maybe more. I served on the rescue team
at Monongah. We found about eighty
and laid them out, like catfish fillets
shriveled up from the heat. Occasionally
I saw something in all that charcoal
that made me remember: There was a man.
I never saw white men cry over Black men
until I worked on that mine rescue team.
I never knew native born men would cry
like those men cried for Polish and Greek,
for Hungarian, Russian, Italian,
and others I might be leaving out.
They say 360 died. That was only the men
whose names they knew how to pronounce.

So many died for coal, whether they died
in the Great Bend Tunnel or in a mine.
Some died in explosions or roof-falls
and never had a chance, and others died
doing stupid things, like slipping on grease,
like Russell Matheny—
crushing his head on a cast-iron pump—
or falling asleep and getting blown up.
But no death is stupid—or all of them are.

I'd bring them all back, even if it meant

no coal to Pittsburgh, Norfolk, or Baltimore.
No coal by rail. No lights, no iron, no steam.
Let there be no coal and no winter heat.
I'd bring them all back, including John.

13. BALTIMORE
(1938?)

I've always been underground—but that can't be.
I'm in Baltimore, no coal mine for miles.

I can look out and see houses with white marble steps,
stretching all the way to North Avenue.
Then, I think—what about Mrs. Hawkins, five doors down?
She breathes hard and has to rest,
leaning against the brick wall of her house.
It's been three days since she's come out.
I wonder if she's all right. So I take a walk
even though Polly yells for me to come back
and mind my own business. When I knock
and that old woman, five doors down,
sticks her head out—Polly's face lights up,
and she yells after me: "Philip, you forgot
that ice tea I made for Mrs. Hawkins."
And at my age, maybe I did forget the tea,
but I won't forget to watch out for who's in danger—
and there's plenty of danger in Baltimore—
sickness, Jim Crow, the police—I watch out
because I've got habits I learned underground.
Polly does too but won't admit it.

14. THE JOHN HENRY SONG

It's a song for pick and shovel men,
for mule skinners, steel drivers, coal miners,
blast-oven and furnace men.

You don't have to be Black
to sing it, and you can be female.
Plenty of women learned to sing the song
by cooking for white folks, tending the sick,
doing field work, working hard as a man,
usually harder. You can be anything you want—
even a singer can sing it, although
most can't.

I don't mean glory work, not the kind of work
that makes you famous, not work
playing a game or writing words
that rhyme or don't rhyme. Just work

on a job where—if the boss wants you
he says, YOU!
and if the wrong fellow looks up
he says, NOT YOU ASS-HOLE!

YOU—
WITH THE BRIGHT BANDANNA!

The kind of work that doesn't pay,
that you curse at the end of the day.

And if you don't know the kind of work I mean,
take a nine-pound hammer
and swing it all day long.
It'll help your singing.

15. WHAT IS YOUR FAVORITE VERSION OF THE BALLAD?

(Phil Henderson laughs—)

Ballad? I don't like the ballads.
But this work song tells the truth

(Phil Henderson sings—)

This old hammer,
Killed John Henry,

This old hammer,
Killed John Henry,

This old hammer,
Killed John Henry,

Killed him dead,
Killed him dead.

(Pause—)

Won't kill us, though,
Won't kill us.

(Phil Henderson laughs)

16. WHAT JOHN AND PHIL TALKED ABOUT

Scholars come to ask about John—
always the same questions.
How tall was he? What did he weigh?
Was he as strong as everyone says?
Did he use one hammer or two?
Did he die racing the steam drill
or shortly after? But they never ask
what John and I talked about
or what we thought.

John Henry and I were barely grown,
but we knew enough to talk about
the slaves that built the pyramids
and what they must have thought and known.

John Henry and I
talked about the future as well as the past.
We talked about everything under the sun.
John Henry had dreams!

David Salner's poetry is deeply influenced by the people he knew during the 25 years he worked at manual trades. An iron ore miner, furnace tender, power plant laborer, machinist, and garment worker, he lived in Minnesota, Arizona, Utah, and for many years in West Virginia,

Before becoming an industrial worker, Salner completed an MFA degree at the University of Iowa Writers' Workshop. The author of three previous books, he received a *Puffin Foundation* grant to study the real history behind the John Henry myth. His work has appeared in *Threepenny Review, Prairie Schooner, The Literary Review, North American Review, Southern Humanities Review, Free Lunch, Poetry Daily,* and many other journals.

In recent years, Salner has taught English as a second language; he currently works as a librarian. He lives in Frederick, MD with his wife, Barbara Greenway, a high school English teacher.

Breinigsville, PA USA
14 October 2010
247341BV00001B/2/P